TABLE OF CONTENTS

ACRONYMS vi

ILLUSTRATIONS vii

TABLES viii

INTRODUCTION 1

OPERATIONAL ENVIRONMENT BACKGROUND 2

LITERATURE REVIEW 5

METHODOLOGY 24

A THEORETICAL FORCE SIZE MODEL 25

OVERVIEW OF SELECTED ENGINEER FORCES 26

POTENTIAL PARTNER NATIONS 29

VIGNETTE 1: GHANA 33

VIGNETTE 2: RWANDA 35

VIGNETTE 3: SENEGAL 36

VIGNETTE 4: TANZANIA 37

CONCLUSION 39

BIBLIOGRAPHY 42

ACRONYMS

ACOTA	African Contingency Operations Training and Assistance
ASF	African Standby Forces
AU	African Union
DOD	Department of Defense
GDP	Gross Domestic Product
MCC	Millenium Challenge Corporation
R2P	Responsibility to Protect
SPP	State Partnership Program

INTRODUCTION

Imagine a world in 2030 where a farmer and his family, who live in the Sahel region, begin to experience the effects of desertification on his farmland. His farmland provides basic sustenance for his family, and he hopes to have a surplus crop that he can sell at the market to obtain the funds necessary to send his children to school in support of his hope that they will enjoy a better life than him. To plant this crop he had to gain access to land, water, and fight other migrant workers who are trying to do the same thing he is doing. Perhaps the sub-Saharan Africa of 2030 sounds farfetched but this situation will become the new normal according to the National Intelligence Council.[1] Despite all of these hurdles the individual faces, there is one remaining challenge. Even if he overcomes the environmental challenges and has excess crop after feeding his family, he finds that he cannot transport his crop to market because there is a degraded road network that precludes him from moving his goods. In another, much more likely, scenario this farmer is forced to move from his land because it is no longer productive. He decides to move to a new urban center because he knows that there is economic growth in cities.[2] However, when he arrives, he finds that this fact is of little comfort because the urban infrastructure in his African city is woefully inadequate in providing the needed water, sewage, telecommunications, or transport for manufactured goods.

The purpose of this monograph is to explore the utility of establishing an African engineer organization, or expand the capacity of existing African engineer units to help the United States indirectly achieve its security interests in sub-Saharan Africa. The United States will leverage its military engineer capabilities to provide training and equipment to selected sub-

---

[1]Office of the Director of National Intelligence Council, *Global Trends 2030: Alternative Worlds,* December 2012. National Intelligence Council, http://www.dni.gov/files/documents/GlobalTrends_ 2030.pdf (accessed October 1, 2013), 14.

[2]Ibid., 10.

1

Saharan African nations. These newly designed African engineer units are designed to be dual-use. This is defined as providing benefits to both the civil population of the nation receiving aid and helping to expand the military capabilities and capacity of the host nation military so this force can better respond to natural disasters, humanitarian crisis, or peace operations. The establishment of these new or enhanced engineer units will indirectly help the United States achieve its broad strategic interests of helping African nations achieve economic prosperity, which provides a foundation for political stability, and it helps African militaries respond to crises as they arise across the continent.

This study will be conducted by first explaining the logic of this proposal within the current operational environment. A literature review will study key areas that affect this proposed security cooperation concept. A methodology will be provided to explain how the qualitative analysis will be conducted. After the methodology, an existing theoretical force size model is examined to explain the desired force size for the sub-Saharan African environments in which American engineer forces will operate. A truth table is provided that highlights which African nations are in a position to benefit from this proposed program. An overview of the sub-Saharan engineer forces is provided to explain why the United States is building or expanding the capabilities of units that already exist. After this, a series of four vignettes will be examined that will explain potential partner nations' infrastructure needs. Finally, the conclusion will discuss results of the study and provide recommendations for future research.

OPERATIONAL ENVIRONMENT BACKGROUND

The contemporary economic realities of sub-Saharan Africa makes it necessary to focus on improving the ability of the state to generate and maintain infrastructure to facilitate economic development activities like regional trade and manufacturing. In sub-Saharan Africa, the state is the driver of economic development. The states have joined regional blocks like the Economic Community of West African States, the East African Community, and various other regional organizations to help foster economic, political, and cultural ties.[3] The formal economy in Africa is characterized by an over-reliance on commodities and a lack of diversity.[4] There is also a large informal economy of trade that occurs within sub-Saharan Africa. This study defines the informal economic sector as economic activities that are not taxed, observed, or regulated by the government. For example, within the South African Development Community, it is estimated that up to $17.6 billion of trade occurs which represents 30-40 percent of that block's trades. Other estimates indicate that informal trading accounts for 20 percent of Gross Domestic Product (GDP) in Nigeria and up to 75 percent in Benin.[5] On one hand, these informal trading networks give Africans a potential for greater economic opportunity, but the revenue generated in these informal exchanges cannot be taxed by the state and reinvested. Furthermore, the potential of this informal network is not being fully realized. Economic studies highlight how regional economies could grow if sufficient infrastructure is available to promote trade. For example, trade within the West African Economic and Monetary Union could increase by three times if all roads linking the various member states were paved.[6] One academic study discovered that if member states were better able to reduce distance between trading partners and maximize trade with neighboring

---

[3]Economic Community of West African States, "Discover ECOWAS," ECOWAS, http://www.comm.ecowas.int/sec/index.php?id=about_a&lang=en (accessed March 17, 2014); East African Community, "About EAC," Corporate Communications and Public Affairs Department, http://www.eac.int/index.php?option=com_content&view=article&id=1&Itemid=53 (accessed March 17, 2014).

[4]United Nations, *Economic Development in Africa Report 2013, Intra-African Trade: Unlocking Private Sector Dynamism,* 2013, United Nations Conference on Trade and Development, http://unctad.org/en/PublicationsLibrary/aldcafrica2013_en.pdf (accessed March 16, 2014), 14.

[5]Ibid., 14-17.

[6]Souleymane Coulibaly and Lionel Fontagné, "South-South Trade: Geography Matters," *Journal of African Economies,* July 8, 2004, CEPII, http://www.cepii.fr/PDF_PUB/wp/2004/wp2004-08.pdf (accessed February 24, 2014), 313-341.

3

countries, then regional trade could expand by up 173 percent.[7] If national and regional infrastructures are sufficiently developed, then these nations will have a way to both increase their economies and obtain additional revenue by formalizing a larger share of their economy.

Regional integration and transportation infrastructure development will be the only way for many sub-Saharan African nations to achieve adequate rates of growth. Of the 54 African nations, many have small national markets. In 2010, it was reported that 24 out of 53 African nations had a population of less than 10 million people and the GDP of 29 countries was less than $10 billion, with 18 countries have a GDP of less than $5 billion. To put this in perspective, many companies have revenues larger than the GDP of these African nations. In 2012, 266 of Fortune 500 companies had revenue streams that exceeded $10 billion.[8] In order to enjoy larger rates of economic growth, the *United Nations Economic Development in Africa Report 2011* recommended that African nations focus on developing their manufacturing capabilities. However, among other areas of concern, African states do not have the proper infrastructure in place to pursue this path.[9]

It is not enough to simply provide new and innovative methods to help African nations develop their infrastructure and help the regional security brigades conduct their missions. The ultimate end is to create a peaceful environment that allows for long-term political stability where people feel secure and prosperous. This will also create additional economic benefit to help boost GDP growth. For example, according to an Oxfam report, from 1990 to 2005, 23 African countries (with the vast majority being in sub-Saharan Africa) lost $284 billion in assets due to

---

[7]Letizia Montinari and Giorgio Prodi, "China's Impact on Intra-African Trade," *The Chinese Economy* 44, no. 4 (August 2011): 80.

[8]United Nations, *Economic Development in Africa Report 2013,* 50.

[9]United Nations, *Economic Development in Africa Report 2011, Fostering Industrial Development in Africa in the New Global Environment,* 2011, United Nations Conference on Trade and Development, http://unctad.org/en/docs/aldcafrica2011_en.pdf (accessed March 16, 2014), 10.

armed conflict.[10] On average, this represents an annual loss of $18 billion or 15 percent of GDP for the nations involved. This total is roughly the amount of all foreign aid given to Africa in the same period.[11] Considering the heavy involvement of the state in African affairs, military involvement is desirable because development aid can be managed and directed by the United States military with inputs from the recipient nations. American engineer forces have gained experience operating in austere environments such as Iraq and Afghanistan. These forces are capable of rendering aid that can overcome the challenges in the sub-Saharan African operational environment.

LITERATURE REVIEW

The following collection of works was selected to provide a foundation for the proposed concept of building engineer capacity. In order to determine the scope of the problem a brief historical and structural examination of infrastructure in sub-Saharan Africa will be conducted. The strategic interests of the United States will be examined to explain why this concept is important in addressing the security interests of the United States. The African regional security brigades will be studied to determine how they provide security on the continent and show how they are a viable vehicle for the United States to use to achieve its security interests. Regional economic development will be studied to determine if targeted American aid has a secondary benefit for regional neighbors. An overview of American aid programs and military organizations is provided to help determine whom and what programs may be used to execute this concept.

---

[10]The nations list in the report are: Algeria, Angola, Burundi, Central African Republic, Chad, Democratic Republic of Congo, Republic of Congo, Côte d'Ivoire, Djibouti, Eritrea, Ethiopia, Ghana, Guinea, Guinea-Bissau, Liberia, Niger, Nigeria, Rwanda, Senegal, Sierra Leone, South Africa, Sudan and Uganda. International Action Network on Small Arms, Briefing Paper 107, *Africa's Missing Billions,* October 2007, Oxfam International, http://www.oxfam.org/sites/www.oxfam.org/files/africas%20missing%20bils.pdf (accessed November 24, 2013), 8-9.

[11]Ibid.

Finally, a brief overview will be provided to show how foreign aid and infrastructure development contribute to political stability.

There are structural and historical trends that place sub-Saharan African nations at a disadvantage in trying to build and maintain an infrastructure that lets these nations participate in the globalized economy. Jeffrey Herbst's work *States and Power in Africa: Comparative Lessons in Authority and Control* helps explain the historical reasons why there is a lack of infrastructure in sub-Saharan Africa when compared to other continental regions such as Europe. Power, in an African context, was not determined by the amount of land one controlled. This was due to the low population density.[12] Indeed, it was not until 1975 that sub-Saharan Africa reached the same level of population density that Europe had in 1500.[13] There was also a lack of resources and incentives that did not lend itself to providing the means necessary to construct an infrastructure network outside the centers of power. Most rulers were content to let members of the hinterland govern themselves as long as tribute was paid.[14] This cultural predisposition was further reinforced by colonial authorities. With the general exception of South Africa, colonial powers did not develop a large network across the vast land network of Africa.[15] Finally, as a generalization, road development across Africa has been poor for those nations who gained independence in the 1960s and 1970s.[16] These factors, when combined, have left many nations in Africa at a significant disadvantage as they try to compete in the twenty-first century globalized economy.

---

[12]Jeffrey Ira Herbst, *States and Power in Africa: Comparative Lessons in Authority and Control*, Princeton Studies in International History and Politics (Princeton, NJ: Princeton University Press, 2000), 36.

[13]Ibid., 16.

[14]Ibid., 42-43.

[15]Ibid., 85.

[16]Ibid., 163.

From a comparative standpoint, sub-Saharan Africa suffers from a lack of infrastructure that has inhibited its ability to fully integrate into the global economy. While there have recently been positive trends much work remains to be done for sub-Saharan Africa to realize its full potential. In most African nations, the lack of infrastructure helps suppress economic growth by up to 40 percent.[17] This negative economic impact is as large as other activities such as crime, corruption, and other bureaucratic inefficiencies.[18] Africa's largest infrastructure deficit occurs in power generation. The combined 48 nations of sub-Saharan Africa produce as much power as the nation of Spain. Per capita power is falling. When viewed on an individual level, there is only enough power available to light a 100 watt light bulb for three hours per day. Africa's available road infrastructure is inadequate when compared to the total land area of the continent. Only one-third of the African population lives within two miles of an all-season road as compared to two-thirds in the rest of developing world.[19]

It is necessary to determine the strategic interests of the United States before American time and treasure are expended in developing an African engineer capability. The strategic justification to establish an organization that is capable of fulfilling the roles described above is found in numerous strategic documents. It will directly support two of the four pillars established in the 2012 *United States Strategy Toward sub-Saharan Africa*. Pillar two establishes the strategic objective to, "Spur Economic Growth, Trade, and Investment."[20] By providing our

---

[17]While the numbers in this source show the poor state of infrastructure in sub-Saharan Africa, they are actually worse. The figures cited include the nation of South Africa which is much more developed than other sub-Saharan African nations. The World Bank, "Fact Sheet: Infrastructure in Sub-Saharan Africa," The World Bank Group, http://web.worldbank.org/WEBSITE/EXTERNAL/COUNTRIES/ AFRICAEXT/0,,contentMDK:21951811~pagePK:146736~piPK:146830~theSitePK:258644,00.html (accessed March 15, 2014).

[18]Ibid.

[19]Ibid.

[20]US President, *United States Strategy Toward Sub-Saharan Africa,* June 2012, The White House. http://www.whitehouse.gov/sites/default/files/docs/africa_strategy_2.pdf (accessed November 8, 2013), 7.

African partners with the ability to expand their economy the United States military and its coalition partners will support the strategies sub-objective of, "Expanding African Capacity to Effectively Access and Benefit from Global Markets."[21] The proposed organization will be structured according to guidelines found in pillar three, "Advance Peace and Security."[22] Specifically, the strategy calls for conducting expanded security cooperation activities in sub-Saharan Africa, but it also emphasizes that these activities must be low-cost and not involve a large United States presence.[23] The ability to have a small engineer presence that is capable of aiding sub-Saharan African nations will help the United States Department of Defense (DOD) achieve its goal of making the United States the, "security partner of choice" across sub-Saharan Africa.[24] These units will also help address the strategic need to provide a rotational presence of American units that will help African militaries develop their capacity and capability. This presence will lead to stronger regional alliances and help increase American influence in sub-Saharan Africa.[25] Finally, these engineer organizations will fulfill some of the objectives laid out in the Africa Command Posture Statement. The two command priorities that this organization will directly affect are "Strengthening Defense Capabilities and Preparing and Responding to Crisis."[26]

---

[21]US President, *United States Strategy Toward Sub-Saharan Africa,* 8.

[22]Ibid.

[23]Ibid., 9.

[24]US President, *Sustaining U.S. Global Leadership: Priorities for 21st Century Defense*, January 2012, US Department of Defense, http://www.defense.gov/news/defense_strategic_guidance.pdf (accessed November 8, 2013), 9.

[25]Ibid., 11.

[26]US Congress, Senate, *Statement of General Carter Hamm USA Commander, US Africa Command before the Senate Armed Services Committee*, March 7, 2013, US Africa Command, http://www.africom.mil/Content/CustomPages/ResearchPage/pdfFiles/2013%20AFRICOM%20Posture%20Statment.pdf (accessed November 8, 2013), 13-18.

The need to develop Africa's infrastructure must be balanced with a realistic appraisal of the assets available to conduct the security cooperation training and equipping. In a recent interview with the Africa Command Commander, General David M. Rodriguez, and Ms. Linda Thomas-Greenfield, Assistant Secretary of the Bureau of African Affairs within the Department of State, Ms. Thomas-Greenfield stated that alleviating poverty and insurgencies without a large degree of infrastructure investment would be impossible. She also noted that the United States does not have the billions of dollars on hand to undertake this task.[27] With this in mind, it is necessary to develop an organization that can utilize the capabilities of multiple military organizations in the most efficient manner possible in order to achieve the two objectives stated above. A way to do this is to increase the percentage of existing aid dollars that go to infrastructure development.

The last strategic justification to build a dual-use engineer capability in Africa is the concept of Responsibility to Protect (commonly referred to as R2P). The concept of R2P is examined in this monograph because the development of African national engineer capabilities will be instrumental in helping populations who are suffering from or have the potential to suffer from genocide or atrocities. R2P has been included in the United States 2010 *National Security Strategy*. The National Security Strategy recognizes that preventing genocide and mass atrocities is in the national interest. To help achieve those ends, the United States will work with organizations such as the African Union (AU) to help empower them to prevent or respond to atrocities or genocide.[28]

---

[27]General David M. Rodriguez and Assistant Secretary Linda Thomas-Greenfield, "TRANSCRIPT: General Rodriguez on Security Cooperation in Sub-Saharan Africa," October 25, 2013, US Africa Command, http://www.africom.mil/Newsroom/Transcript/11406/general-rodriguez-on-security-cooperation-in-sub-saharan-africa (accessed November 8, 2013).

[28]US President, *National Security Strategy*, May 2010, The White House, http://www.whitehouse.gov/sites/default/files/rss_viewer/national_security_strategy.pdf (accessed November 16, 2013), 48.

While the National Security Strategy establishes the strategic interest to prevent genocide, it is necessary to look to other documents to help explain how the United States military can operationalize this concept. Former Secretary of State, Madeline K. Albright and former presidential envoy to Sudan, Richard S. Williamson created a document to help guide the development of programs that can help counter genocide. They note in *The United States and R2P: From Words to Action*, that R2P is based upon three pillars. The first is that it is the duty of every state to protect its people; the second is that the international community must help states protect their citizens; and finally, it is the duty of the international community to take action if the state in question is failing to protect its citizens.[29] The engineer organization being described is a way to provide a capability that adequately addresses the strategic interests stated in the National Security Strategy. An engineer organization will provide a capability that will help African nations address the operational challenges that are present when a mission is conducted to prevent or respond to a mass atrocity. Finally, if authorized by the AU, this engineer organization will empower AU security brigades. The standby brigades will provide an international response force if needed. While all three pillars are addressed, emphasis is placed on the first two. While it does not provide sensational coverage on the evening news, prevention is much more desirable than responding to a crisis. As Ambassador Albright and Special Envoy Williamson note, "The preventive responsibilities inherent in the first two pillars of R2P are best reflected not in the emergencies that attract publicity but in the quiet progress that does not."[30]

---

[29]Madeline Albright and Richard Williamson, "The United States and R2P: From Words to Action," The United States Institute of Peace, the United States Holocaust Memorial Museum, and the Brookings Institutue, 2013, http://www.brookings.edu/~/media/Research/Files/Papers/2013/07/23 %20united%20states%20responsibility%20protect%20albright%20williamson/23%20united%20states%20 responsibility%20protect%20albright%20williamson.pdf (accessed November 16, 2013), 10.

[30]Albright and Williamson, 14.

It is necessary to keep the African security brigades in mind if the United States decides to work with our African partners to build an enhanced African engineer capability. While engineer forces will be developed at the national level they should be purposefully designed through their training and equipping for regional integration with other sub-Saharan nations. This is due to the fact that when sub-Saharan African nations deploy military forces for peace operations these forces are designed to act as part of a regional security apparatus that roughly parallels the regional economic blocs. These regional military forces are called the African Standby Forces (ASF). The AU proposed the creation of five regional security brigades to respond to crises across the continent. The brigades are comprised of both military and civilian members. The brigades have been designed to respond to a range of mission sets. These mission sets include acting as regional military advisors to an AU or United Nations political mission, deploying as a stand-alone AU force for peace operations, deploying on a United Nations sponsored mission, or acting as an intervention force.[31]

The geographic distribution of the regional brigades are outlined in figure 1 and a proposed order of battle is highlighted in figure 2. While the ASF seems promising, the organizations have encountered numerous challenges that make their full development problematic. There is uneven development across the regions; the brigades suffer from logistical shortfalls; many African nations lack the resources to properly equip the brigade; and there are funding problems for prolonged operations.[32] While the ASF force may not come to its full theoretical fruition it does provide a baseline from which African forces could develop. In principle, this has already occurred. Many nations from the Economic Community of West

---

[31]Billy Batware, "The African Standby Force A Solution to African Conflicts?" European Peace University, December 19, 2011, Academic, http://www.academia.edu/3402412/The_African_Standby_Force_A_Solution_to_African_Conflicts (accessed January 2, 2014), 5.

[32]Batware, 9-14.

African States provided soldiers to help stabilize Mali before the United Nations took over the mission. Nigeria, Benin, Ghana, Niger, Senegal, Guinea, Burkina Faso and Togo provided approximately 3,300 soldiers to the African-led International Support to Mali.[33] The adopted order of battle is just a starting point. Particularly for scenario five, engineer forces that are able to construct and maintain roads and provide power would prove a crucial enabler for humanitarian assistance or disaster relief. The key point for the ASF is that African political authorities have committed to build a military organization that can take of care of African problems when they erupt. This ASF provides a vehicle for the United States to achieve its strategic interests and it helps the AU increase the capabilities of the African Security Brigades to help African nations solve their own internal problems and achieve higher levels of regional integration.

[33]BBC, "African Troops for Mali 'in Days,'" January 15, 2013, British Broadcasting Corporation, http://www.bbc.co.uk/news/world-africa-21029916 (accessed January 3, 2014).

Figure 1. African Security Brigades

Source: Billy Batware, "The African Standby Force A Solution to African Conflicts?" European Peace University, December 19, 2011, Academia, http://www.academia.edu/3402412/The_ African_Standby_Force_A_Solution_to_African_Conflicts (accessed January 2, 2014), 4.

Figure 2. Notional ASF Order of Battle

Source: Billy Batware, "The African Standby Force A Solution to African Conflicts?" European Peace University, December 19, 2011, Academia, http://www.academia.edu/3402412/The_ African_Standby_Force_A_Solution_to_African_Conflicts (accessed January 2, 2014), 4.

Bougheas, Demetriades and Morgenroth demonstrate the impacts on regional economies of domestic investment in infrastructure in their piece "International Aspects of Public Infrastructure Investment." The authors of this study build a two-country model that examines infrastructure investment impacts on domestic and international trade by reducing transportation costs. This model is then tested by examining data from 16 European states from 1987-1995. Measures examined were roads, railways, maritime ports, and airports. Their model produced positive results. For example, it shows a positive impact for the GDP of Belgium due to France's decision to invest in its infrastructure. The French will benefit from their own internal decision,

14

but there is a benefit to its neighbors as well.[34] The impact of the economic benefit will be influenced by factors such as a nation's population, debt ratio, population density, and current GDP; but in general the study shows the positive impacts of a national decision to invest in infrastructure. More importantly, using this model, it also shows that by using a regional investment strategy it is theoretically possible to achieve better economic outcomes.[35]

The importance of regional investment in infrastructure is recognized by the Center of Global Development. In the essay, "Power and Roads for Africa," Vijaya Ramachandran highlights the need for investment in two key areas: power infrastructure and roads. Without investment in these two areas, the development of the private sector will be hampered and it will be virtually impossible to establish a healthy business environment.[36] With approximately one-sixth of the world's population, Africa only accounts for 4 percent of world power output with the majority of this total being used in South Africa and the north African nations. Biomass, mostly in the form of firewood, constitutes approximately 56 percent of energy use in sub-Saharan Africa. This type of energy use leads to an acceleration of deforestation. Businesses cope with this lack of power supply by relying heavily on generators. While this method provides power, it is highly inefficient and puts African businesses at a competitive disadvantage in the marketplace. For example, energy as a total share of business expense is 10 percent in Africa whereas in China energy it is only 3 percent.[37] A lack of transportation infrastructure in Africa means that businesses are only able to sell their goods in regional markets or markets that ensure a high

---

[34]Spiros Bougheas, Panicos O. Demetriades, and Edgar L. W. Morgenroth, "International Aspects of Public Infrastructure Investment," *The Canadian Journal of Economics / Revue canadienne d'Economique* 36, no. 4 (November 1, 2003): 884-910, http://www.jstor.org/stable/3131805 (accessed September 19, 2013).

[35]Ibid., 903-904.

[36]Vijaya Ramachandran, "Power and Roads for Africa," March 2008, Center for Global Development, www.cgdev.org/content/publications/detail/15659 (accessed October 14, 2014), 3.

[37]Ibid., 4-6.

profit margin to overcome the high cost of transportation.[38] This piece, and others already examined, have highlighted the positive results of investing in infrastructure and have described the existing state of sub-Sahran African infrastructure. The next step is to examine current aid programs to see how the United States military can help African nations develop their national infrastructure and provide support to the security brigades.

The Congressional Research Report *U.S. Foreign Assistance to Sub-Saharan Africa: The FY2012 Request* provides an overview of major categories of foreign aid to sub-Saharan Africa. The United States devotes over one-quarter of its entire foreign aid budget, or approximately $7.8 billion, to sub-Saharan Africa. This total does not include Millennium Challenge Corporation (MCC) funding. Seventy-four percent of total funds goes toward efforts to combat diseases such as malaria and HIV/AIDS. Other large areas of categories of investment are economic growth which receives $1.1 billion (15 perccent of total aid), peace and security which receives $430.8 million (6 percent of total aid), and efforts to strengthen democratic institutions which receives $371.3 million (5 percent of total aid). Direct funding for infrastructure projects constitutes a small portion of the economic aid budget at $82.7 million (~1 percent of total aid). This represents a 35.4 percent decrease from fiscal year 2010. The majority of these funds were concentrated in South Sudan. No large-scale aid was given to enhance African military engineer efforts. Peace and security funds were used for force professionalization, mitigating armed conflict, counterterror programs, counternarcotic programs, maritime security, and participation in multilateral exercises.[39]

---

[38]Ramachandran, 7.

[39]Alexis Arieff, Nicolas Cook, Lauren Ploch, Tiaji Salaam-Blyther, Alexandra Kendall, Curt Tarnoff, and Melissa D. Ho, Congressional Research Service Report for Congress, *U.S. Foreign Assistance to Sub-Saharan Africa: The FY2012 Request,* May 20, 2011, Federation of American Scientists, http://www.fas.org/sgp/crs/row/R41840.pdf (accessed October 14, 2013), 10-21.

The MCC has provided large amounts of monetary assets to help foreign governments with large-scale infrastructure projects. MCC differs from other forms of aid because it mandates that foreign governments plan for and implement projects on their own. Approximately 58 percent of $8.4 billion given in aid, or $4.8 billion, has been given to African nations. Many of these projects have emphasized infrastructure development. The MCC is also valuable because it has a vetting process that helps ensure that large-scale projects can be completed and used to their full potential. The MCC website states, "For a country to be selected as eligible for an MCC assistance program, it must demonstrate a commitment to just and democratic governance, investments in its people, and economic freedom as measured by different policy indicators."[40] Despite the billions of dollars being spent on aid for Africa, it is reported that American influence could be challenged in Africa. In 2012, China committed to provide $20 billion in loans for agriculture and infrastructure development. While this level of aid is roughly the same in monetary terms, the Chinese aid is concentrated far more in areas that help African nations promote economic growth.[41] In order to reach this level of infrastructure aid, virtually all of the existing United States aid budget would have to be transitioned from disease relief and disease prevention to infrastructure and economic development. While this is unlikely to occur, the DOD can plan its security cooperation efforts to supplement existing interagency programs like the MCC and increase the American ability to help African nations build their needed infrastructure.

In order for the United States military to partner with African militaries to enhance their capabilities to improve infrastructure and regional security organizations, it is necessary to ensure that the United States military operates under appropriate authorities and funding sources. In the

---

[40]Millenium Challenge Corporation, "Selection Criteria," http://www.mcc.gov/pages/ selection (accessed October 14, 2013).

[41]Nancy Birdsall and Alexis Sowa, "From Multilateral Champion to Handicapped Donor - And Back Again?" *PRISM* 4, no. 3 (2013): 81-82.

security cooperation environment there are many programs that one can consider. One of the most recently developed programs that offers the most promise is the 1206 program. This program is described by Nina Serafino in the Congressional Research Service report *Security Assistance Reform: "Section 1206" Background and Issues for Congress*. In its current form the 1206 Program is primarily designed to support foreign militaries to perform counterterrorism operations through train and equip programs. The second aim of the program is to enable selected foreign militaries to participate in stability operations in areas where United States military forces are operating. While this program shares similarities with other programs such as the Foreign Military Sales or Foreign Military Finance programs, it offers distinct advantages. In general, Foreign Military Sales or Foreign Military Finance programs take three to four years to come to fruition and must undergo a laborious process of approval. The 1206 process can be accomplished in one year or less. Additionally, the 1206 Program is under the lead authority of the DOD. This enables the DOD to exercise control of the program for areas in which it has expertise. It is important to note that the 1206 Program is a "dual key program."[42] This means that concurrence from the State Department must be obtained before aid can be rendered.[43] While the 1206 Program offers a good template, its existing authorities would need to be expanded or a new program created in a similar fashion that provides engineering units the ability to rapidly train and equip a nation's engineer assets to enhance their capabilities. An expanded 1206 Program would complement other efforts being undertaken to develop infrastructure by organizations such as the United States Agency for International Development. Legislative authority was granted in the 2013 National Defense Authorization Act to allow 1206 funds to be used for small-scale

---

[42]Nina Serafino, Congressional Research Service Report for Congress, *Security Assistance Reform: 'Section 1206' Background and Issues for Congress*, April 19, 2013, Federation of American Scientists, http://www.fas.org/sgp/crs/natsec/RS22855.pdf (accessed November 14, 2013), 10.

[43]Ibid., 10.

construction projects in support of contingency operations.[44] While this authority does not meet the needs for a proposed organization like the one articulated in this monograph, it does show a willingness by Congress to expand the needed authorities. If the benefit of this program is clearly articulated, then the means can be generated to support its creation.

The United States military has a variety of engineer organizations and programs at its disposal to help conduct engineer security cooperation activities in the focus areas already mentioned. The organizations and their capabilities are described in Joint Publication 3-34, *Joint Engineer Operations*. The five focus areas described in this monograph are considered General Engineering Tasks. Figure 4 describes these tasks in detail.[45] Appendix B in Joint Publication 3-34 lists the organizations that will undertake these operations. Army general engineering support missions are performed by four types of organization. These are the horizontal construction company, the vertical construction company, multi-role bridge company, and an engineer support company.[46] As stated earlier, the emphasis of this program is to establish a core capability of road construction and maintenance and facilities construction. With that in mind, the focus will be on examining those capabilities that can be synthesized from the American horizontal and vertical construction companies. Joint Publication 3-34 provides the following description of these two organizations:

> The horizontal and vertical companies have a construction focus and are capable of constructing, rehabilitating, repairing, maintaining, and modifying landing strips, airfields, CPs, MSRs, supply installations, building structures, bridges, and other related aspects of the infrastructure. These units may also perform repairs and limited

---

[44]US Congress, 19-20.

[45]Joint Chiefs of Staff (JCS), Joint Publication (JP) 3-34, *Joint Engineer Operations* (Washington, DC: US Government Printing Office, 2011), IV-5 to IV-6.

[46]Ibid., B-A-4.

reconstruction of railroads or water and sewage facilities. The basic capabilities of these construction units can be expanded significantly.[47]

Once fully trained, these units can be augmented with additional assets or work with other enablers to execute more advanced engineering tasks. The Army can also provide support to training in power generation. The Prime Power Detachment is a specialized capability that can help train African engineer units in how to produce power and distribute it to customers. This organization can also conduct electrical surveys and show African engineer units how to maintain electrical power equipment.[48] Power generation provides an obvious benefit. When not being utilized for contingency missions or humanitarian assistance, this capability could be used to help develop the national infrastructure. This military effort would supplement an existing program being executed by the United States Agency for International Development in conjunction with other partners like the World Bank, the African Development Bank, and various private sector firms. This program is called Power Africa. This program's goal is to add 10,000 megawatts of energy by using wind, solar, hydropower, natural gas, and geothermal sources. This program is being executed in six sub-Saharan African nations. They are Ethiopia, Ghana, Kenya, Liberia, Nigeria, and Tanzania.[49] The United States Army Corps of Engineers is already involved in this program on a limited basis. It charges to provide assistance and management for power projects.[50]

It is assumed that the Army will be the largest contributing force to the engineer development effort. This is based off the size of Army engineer assets and the number of existing programs that can be leveraged to conduct security cooperation in Africa. For example, the

---

[47]Ibid., B-A-5.

[48]JCS, JP 3-34, B-A-5.

[49]US Agency for International Development, *Power Africa, Leveraging Partnerships to Increase Access to Power in Sub-Saharan Africa,* March 26, 2014, http://www.usaid.gov/sites/default/files/ documents/1860/power-africa-overview.pdf (accessed April 11, 2014), 1.

[50]US Agency for International Development, "U.S. Government Agencies," USAID, http://www.usaid.gov/powerafrica/partners/us-government-agencies (accessed May 11, 2014).

United States Army Corps of Engineers has almost 800 uniform military personnel and 35,000 civilians in its workforce. This force works with approximately 300,000 contractors to execute various construction projects.[51] In addition to the United States Army Corps of Engineers, the active Army has initiated a regionally aligned force program to conduct security cooperation efforts. This program does not deal exclusively with engineers, but they are part of it. The National Guard has the State Partnership Program (SPP) that is especially useful for this security cooperation endeavor. The SPP began in 1992 and involves nearly every state and territory of the United States. One of the primary benefits to this program is the enduring relationships it fosters between United States National Guard personnel and members of the partner nation. The SPP is a military program but is comprised of part-time military members who can bring their civilian expertise to bear on a situation. While assessment tools are limited for this program, the studies that exist are encouraging. Of 41 ambassadors who responded to questions on the SPP, 40 reported that it helped the country team reach its goals and objectives.[52] Currently, there are eight African nations participating in the program. The following is a list of states and their African partners. California partnered with Nigeria; New York partnered with South Africa; North Carolina partnered with Botswana; North Dakota partnered with Ghana; Michigan partnered with Liberia; Utah (South Carolina) partnered with Morocco; Vermont partnered with Senegal; and Wyoming partnered with Tunisia.[53]

---

[51]US Army Corps of Engineers, "USACE Overview," US Army Corps of Engineers Headquarters, http://www.usace.army.mil/Portals/2/docs/USACE_101_April_2013.pdf (accessed January 2, 2014).

[52]Lawrence Kapp and Nina Serafino, Congressional Research Service Report for Congress, *The National Guard State Partnership Program: Background, Issues, and Options for Congress,* August 15, 2011, Federation of American Scientists, https://www.fas.org/sgp/crs/misc/R41957.pdf (accessed January 2, 2014), 16.

[53]US Africa Command, "National Guard State Partnership Program," USAFRICOM, http://www.africom.mil/what-we-do/security-cooperation-programs/national-guard (accessed January 2, 2014).

The Navy can also provide significant force capability to aid with engineer security cooperation activities. There are approximately 16,000 naval forces engaged in engineer activities in the active and reserve components.[54] The Naval Mobile Construction Battalions are an extremely versatile force that can conduct the following missions: heavy horizontal and vertical construction capabilities; construct, maintain, and provide bridging support for roads and for supply routes; build expeditionary airfields and advanced bases; maintain airfield pavement; and construct base facilities. This organization can be task organized for specific missions.[55] Considering that security cooperation activities are relatively limited duration missions this is extremely helpful when training on a specific skillset.

The Air Force can help sub-Saharan African nations with airfield construction and maintenance. They do this through their Prime Base Engineer Emergency Force and Rapid Engineer Deployable Heavy Operational Repair Squadron, Engineering. Prime Base Engineer Emergency Force units are lighter than Rapid Engineer Deployable Heavy Operational Repair Squadron, Engineering units but are still capable of conducting site surveys, limited horizontal and vertical construction, concrete and asphalt paving activities, utility system installation and maintenance, installation, geospatial information services, airfield damage repair, and emergency services functions. Rapid Engineer Deployable Heavy Operational Repair Squadron, Engineering capabilities include all of those listed for Prime Base Engineer Emergency Force but they are capable of conducting heavier horizontal and vertical construction activities. Rapid Engineer Deployable Heavy Operational Repair Squadron, Engineering units are also self-sustaining when deployed.[56] Marine Corps forces do have engineer forces, but they are designed to be

---

[54]JCS, JP 3-34, B-B-2.

[55]Ibid., B-B-4 to B-B-5.

[56]Ibid., B-C-1 to B-C-4.

expeditionary in nature. Their capability to provide general engineering support is very limited. By design, when a need for general engineering support emerges then Marine Corps units are augmented with Naval Mobile Construction Battalions.[57]

While the establishment of new engineer units will not directly achieve political stability by itself, it must demonstrate how it contributes to this end through existing academic literature. Byman notes in his study, "Understanding Proto-Insurgencies," that insurgents use geography to their advantage. In remote areas that are hard to access, such as jungles and mountains, insurgents have an environment that allows them to resupply and rest. These areas are easier to defend against host nation police and counterintelligence resources.[58] "The Collier-Hoeffler Model of Civil War," by Paul Collier, Anke Hoeffler, and Nicholar Sambanis explains some of the conditions that exist that provide opportunities for insurgencies to grow. In general, insurgencies are inexpensive. Recruits are generally paid half the money that can be found in peaceful environments; they typically occur in areas that experience low economic growth; they are exacerbated by low capabilities of host nation military forces; and forests and mountains are terrain that aid the insurgent conduct their activities.[59]

Two other studies examine the link between economic growth, foreign aid, and political stability. Stephen Armah examined 31 sub-Saharan African nations from 1984-2007. He found that foreign aid and political stability are closely associated with economic growth. Economic aid promotes growth when it is given to nations that are deemed politically stable. He also finds that the effect of aid is much more limited in nations that are politically unstable. Foreign aid can help

---

[57]JCS, JP 3-34, B-D-2 to B-D-3.

[58]Daniel Byman, RAND Counterinsurgency Study Occasional Paper 3, "Understanding Proto-Insurgencies," National Defense Research Institute, 2007, RAND Corporation, http://www.rand.org/content/dam/rand/pubs/occasional_papers/2007/RAND_OP178.pdf (accessed November 24, 2013), 16.

[59]Paul Collier and Nicholas Sambanis, eds., *Understanding Civil War: Evidence and Analysis,* vol. 1 (Washington, DC: World Bank, 2005), 3-6.

ameliorate immediate problems like starvation but it cannot help with economic growth.[60] Burcu Savun and Daniel Tirone demonstrate that foreign aid can help manage the risk or conflict when lesser-developed countries suffer from an economic shock such as falling agricultural prices. This study demonstrates that small amounts of foreign aid can help prevent the onset of conflict.[61] The literature indicates that an enhanced military engineer capability, when combined with other programs, has the potential to help enhance the economic opportunities in nations where the necessary economic conditions exist and it can help support efforts to solve pressing short-term problems such as a humanitarian crisis or natural disaster.

METHODOLOGY

The proposal will be tested by examining a set of four vignettes to determine the efficacy of establishing a dual-use African engineer capability. The first section describes an existing theoretical model that explains the desired force size. Next, a truth table and a narrative are introduced that help explain the process for selecting these African nations. The truth table is presented in table 1. This force size will be large enough to achieve the stated objectives, but small enough to mitigate the risk of appearing to unduly influence the host nation or appear to be an occupying power. The third section describes the status of engineer forces in each of the nations examined. This study will then examine four nations to determine if these poorer nations have the potential to achieve high levels of growth if external engineer support is provided. This method will be explained in detail in the potential partner nations section. Finally, the results of the vignettes will be examined in the conclusion section and recommendations for future research will be made.

---

[60]Stephen E. Armah, "Investigating the Influence of Political Stability of the Aid-Growth Relationship in Sub-Saharan Africa: A Panel Data Approach," *Journal of Economic Development, Management, IT, Finance, and Marketing* 2, no. 2 (September 2009): 32-56.

[61]Burcu Savun and Daniel C. Tirone, "Exogenous Shocks, Foreign Aid, and Civil War," *International Organization* 66, no. 3 (Summer 2012): 389.

A THEORETICAL FORCE SIZE MODEL

The study adopts Edelstein's model of force size and intervention to highlight the desired benefit of a small force that remains in the background to the largest extent possible (please see figure 3). As the literature review highlights, small amounts of aid and having a small force package can have a large impact on mitigating the risk of a potential crisis. The goals of this proposed security cooperation program are modest. It seeks to build a specific tactical capability in order to accomplish two discrete objectives: (1) helping the host nation develop its infrastructure during peace time in order to contribute to economic growth which promotes stability; and (2) providing a capable engineer force that can be used with the African Security Brigades to help respond to crises across the continent. The proposed train and equip mission is relatively low cost and can be established using a series of existing programs and authorities that do not require a large force structure of American military members.

Figure 3. Security Cooperation Development Risk Model Based on Force Size

Source: Billy Batware, "The African Standby Force A Solution to African Conflicts?" European Peace University, December 19, 2011, Academia, http://www.academia.edu/3402412/The_ African_Standby_Force_A_Solution_to_African_Conflicts (accessed January 2, 2014), 4.

Table 1 lists the four nations that are examined in this monograph in the lower left quadrant. The desired outcome for these nations is high growth of infrastructure if external resources are applied. In general, nations that fall into this category have shown many positive trends recently in economic growth, rule of law, and governance. However, they still require substantial investment to build up their infrastructure. The other nations listed are not considered for analysis. Nations such as South Africa have achieved a high level of development and would not significantly benefit from enhancing their military engineer capacity. While impoverished, the other countries listed are not suitable candidates for a variety of reasons. They are not part of multiple American aid programs and these nations have sanctions issued against them.

Table 1. Truth Table of Short-Term Infrastructure Growth Potential
if External Resources are Made Available

		External Resources Available	
		Yes	No
Growth of short term potential	Low	South Africa	Zimbabwe
	High	Tanzania, Ghana, Senegal, and Rwanda	Sudan

Source: Created by author.

OVERVIEW OF SELECTED ENGINEER FORCES

Three of the four nations examined have an engineer capability as part of their national Army's organization. Table 2 lists published engineer capabilities for the African nations selected for analysis. Naturally, one may ask the question, why would the United States strive to develop this capability if it already exists? However, one must dig deeper than the published strength; what is on paper and actual capability are two different things. As a generalization, the nations listed above have a very limited ability to provide engineer support either to the host nation or to

26

the African Security Force to which they are assigned. An open source assessment of the engineer battalions listed above was not available. While this presents a challenge in trying to directly explain a lack of capability, indirect methods can be utilized to describe the general trends in training and equipment of sub-Saharan African militaries. To achieve this, an interview with a retired Foreign Area Officer with experience in sub-Saharan Africa was conducted and various defense materials were consulted.

Many sub-Saharan African militaries rely heavily upon the donations of military material from more developed nations in order to provide equipment to their forces. When received, some of this equipment may fall into a state of disrepair due to a lack of funds to purchase parts or even provide something as simple as fuel. A former African Foreign Area Officer recalls the story of 10 2.5 trucks (commonly referred to as the deuce and a half) that were donated to the Nigeriens from excess defense articles. Since Niger is a landlocked nation, it was necessary to have these trucks shipped to a port on the Gulf of Guinea and then drive them to Niger. While the Nigeriens were motivated, professional, and appreciated the equipment, it was impossible for them to drive the equipment due to a lack of funds for diesel fuel. During the course of the donation, a separate line item had to be programmed that allowed the Nigeriens to purchase fuel for the drive from the coast to Niger. He also tells a story of the very limited number of C-130s Niger possessed. These platforms were used to connect remote airstrips with the capital of Niamey. Without this precious commodity, the government in Niamey would not have been able to provide supplies to a small number of forces that operated at remote bases in the northeast of the nation. Due to the resource constrained environment, specialized military capabilities such as engineers, aviation, and logistics units that are capable of conducting operations are treated as national asset. These assets help these governments overcome the tyranny of distance.[62]

---

[62]Douglas Lathrop, Retired African Foreign Area Officer, interview by author, March 28, 2014, Fort Leavenworth, KS.

Jane's assessments provide a very limited amount of information on the current capabilities of the engineer units being examined. For example, the country report on Tanzania states that a commitment was made in 2007 to ensure that the Tanzania People's Defense Force had maintenance ability for all equipment.[63] There are indications that African countries will use their military engineer assets for infrastructure development. Jane's reported that Ghana's Defense Minister made a statement in 2010 to establish an additional engineer regiment in the north of the country to help with infrastructure development. This report has not been verified.[64]

No information was provided on significant operational achievements or completed projects. However, despite the training and resource shortfalls, there are relationships and existing engineer activities to build upon. For example, the North Dakota Army and Air Force National Guard have provided a limited amount of engineer training with the Ghanaians. These training events include engineer instructor exchanges, engineer operations, combat engineer familiarization, and building rehabilitation for the Ghanaian government.[65] Other examples include United States Navy Seabees partnering with 15 Ghanaian engineers to construct a medical clinic.[66] Finally, the Senegalese Army worked with the United States Army Corps of

---

[63]IHS Jane's, *Jane's Sentinel Security Assessment - Central Africa, Tanzania.* July 29, 2013, IHS, Inc., https://janes.ihs.com/CustomPages/Janes/DisplayPage.aspx?DocType=Reference&ItemId=+++ 1302683&Pubabbrev=CAF (accessed March 20, 2014), 5.

[64]IHS Jane's, *Jane's Sentinel Security Assessment - Central Africa, Ghana.* July 29, 2013, IHS, Inc., https://janes.ihs.com/CustomPages/Janes/DisplayPage.aspx?DocType=Reference&ItemId=+++ 1305473&Pubabbrev=WAFR (accessed March 20, 2014), 5-6.

[65]North Dakota Office of the Adjutant General, *2009-2011 Biennial Report,* National Guard North Dakota, http://www.ndguard.ngb.army.mil/jointforce/Documents/NDNG-2009-11-Biennial-Report.pdf (accessed March 31, 2014), 15, 49.

[66]US European Command, "Africa Partnership Station Delivers Gift of Hope to Ghana," March 7, 2008, http://www.eucom.mil/article/20633/africa-partnership-station-delivers-gift-hope (accessed March 31, 2014).

Engineers on a major project to improve its training facilities in Dodji. This facility supports 1,000 Soldiers.[67]

Table 2. Current Engineer Capability of Selected Sub-Saharan African Militaries

Source: International Institute for Strategic Studies. *The Military Balance 2012* (New York: Routledge, 2012), 437, 448-450, 456-457.

POTENTIAL PARTNER NATIONS

Potential partner nations are chosen for their demonstrated ability to capitalize on development aid that is given to them. This potential is determined by incorporating programs that rely on high levels of development and governance indicators. Other military programs are also considered. By using these programs as a screening criteria, military planners will ensure that proposed development efforts to build a dual-use engineer capability are nested with participation with other major development programs. It is designed this way to create a compounding effect with other development programs and it will help overcome the stovepiping effect that is produced when aid is given in a disorganized fashion across multiple agencies and military organizations. Civilian and military planners can use numerous methods to crosswalk African nations within existing aid programs to help determine suitable partner nations. An analysis of four aid sources is conducted to ensure unity of effort is achieved. The MCC, Power Africa, and

---

[67]Jennifer Aldridge, "US Upgrades Senegalese Army Training Center," US Army Corps of Engineers, last modified September 13, 2013, http://www.usace.army.mil/Media/NewsArchive/StoryArticleView/tabid/232/Article/18243/us-upgrades-senegalese-army-training-center.aspx (accessed March 31, 2014).

the State Partnership Program have been described. The African Contingency Operations Training and Assistance (ACOTA) is included in this analysis. This is due to the large number of relationships the United States has developed or deepened by operating under this program and the large impact it has had on peacekeeping operations. Since its inception in 1997, ACOTA has trained approximately 254,228 African peacekeepers from 25 African nations.[68]

The four nations considered for qualitative analysis are Ghana, Rwanda, Senegal, and Tanzania due to their participation in the aforementioned programs.[69] Ghana and Senegal participate in the MCC, SPP, and ACOTA programs. Ghana and Tanzania are members of the Power Africa program. Tanzania and Rwanda participate in the MCC and ACOTA programs. In addition to their participation in major development programs, Ghana, Senegal, and Tanzania have hosted regional exercises with the United States. In 2013, Ghana hosted Western Accord 13, Senegal hosted a Special Operations Forces' exercise in 2011 named Flintlock, and Tanzania hosted Eastern Accord in 2012.[70] The pool of selected nations also provides geographical diversity across sub-Saharan Africa. Senegal and Ghana are located in western Africa while Tanzania and Rwanda are located eastern Africa. Rwanda also provides a unique case due to the

---

[68]US Department of State, "African Contingency Operations Training and Assistance ACOTA Program," Press Release|Fact Sheet, last modified February 6, 2013, The Office of Website Management, Bureau of Public Affairs, http://www.state.gov/r/pa/prs/ps/2013/02/203841.htm (accessed February 22, 2014).

[69]African MCC nations were obtained from the following source: Millennium Challenge Corporation, "Participating MCC Nations in Africa," http://www.mcc.gov/pages/countries/region/africa (accessed January 3, 2014). African SPP nations were obtained from: US Africa Command, "National Guard State Partnership Program." Participating members of ACOTA were obtained from: US Department of State, "African Contingency Operations Training and Assistance ACOTA Program."

[70]US Army Africa, "Western Accord 13 Begins Command Post Exercise," http://www.usaraf.army.mil/NEWS/NEWS_130628_wa2.html (accessed March 27, 2014); Major Bryan Purtell, "Flintlock 11 Kicks Off February 21 in Senegal/Media Opportunities," February 3, 2011, Special Operations Command Africa Public Affairs, US Africa Command, http://www.africom.mil/Newsroom/Article/7979/flintlock-11-kicks-off-february-21-in-senegal-medi (accessed March 27, 2014); Captain Michelle Matthews, "Missouri Guardsmen Participate in Eastern Accord Exercise Kick off," September 6, 2012, Missouri National Guard, http://www.moguard.com/09-06-12-missouri-guardsmen-participate-in-eastern-accord-exercise-kick-off.html (accessed March 27, 2014).

fact it is relatively small and it is landlocked. Four vignettes will be developed from this list of nations to determine if developing a military engineer capability will have a positive impact on developing national infrastructure and contributing to the capabilities of the African Security Brigades. These nations are selected for their potential ability to experience short-term economic growth if American military engineer assets are provided. Table 3 shows the road density as compared to the surface area of the countries examined. Road density will be considered with the results of the qualitative analysis to show if the development of a military engineer capability will have any significant impact on an African nation's ability to develop its national infrastructure.

Total net official development assistance is provided to highlight the total amount of foreign aid. This will be used as part of the study to highlight the potential for new road construction within that nation using the construction costs provided in the table 4 below. Distance calculations will be made using the average for large-scale projects of greater than 50 km in order to achieve the greatest degree of surface transportation generation. As a planning factor, this study only uses 20 percent of available aid dollars. This low percentage used is because aid falls into numerous categories such as humanitarian relief, health sector development, etc., and not all of it can be used for infrastructure development. The median figure for road construction per kilometer per lane (km) is $290,639. In order to construct a two-lane highway this study doubles the figure to $581,278. This number will be divided against the total amount of available aid that is assumed. Again, the goal is only to demonstrate the potential for infrastructure development and is not meant to be authoritative. It is up to political and civil organizations to determine appropriate distribution percentages by category.

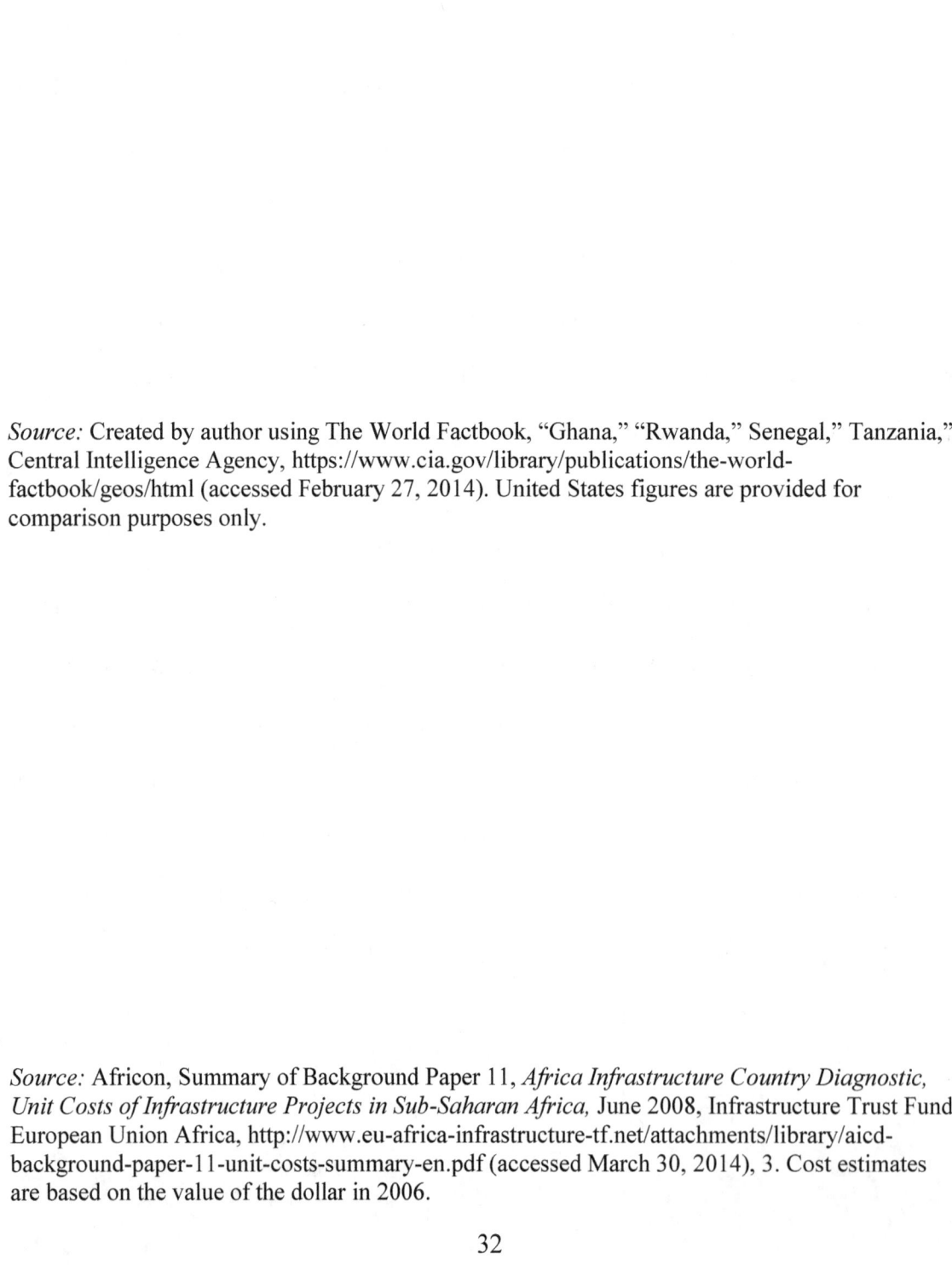

Source: Created by author using The World Factbook, "Ghana," "Rwanda," Senegal," Tanzania," Central Intelligence Agency, https://www.cia.gov/library/publications/the-world-factbook/geos/html (accessed February 27, 2014). United States figures are provided for comparison purposes only.

Source: Africon, Summary of Background Paper 11, *Africa Infrastructure Country Diagnostic, Unit Costs of Infrastructure Projects in Sub-Saharan Africa,* June 2008, Infrastructure Trust Fund European Union Africa, http://www.eu-africa-infrastructure-tf.net/attachments/library/aicd-background-paper-11-unit-costs-summary-en.pdf (accessed March 30, 2014), 3. Cost estimates are based on the value of the dollar in 2006.

VIGNETTE 1: GHANA

Ghana has experienced large amounts of success over the past decade, but still faces many challenges. Ghana is the second largest economy in West Africa and 12th on the continent. It receives high marks in governance and has enjoyed a tremendous rate in GDP growth due to its exports of commodities.[71] Freedom House ranks it as only one of three nations in West Africa to be free (the other two being Senegal and Benin).[72] One of the major impediments to prosperity is Ghana's infrastructure. Despite its political and economic success, Ghana ranks far below Africa's leaders in infrastructure development. In a recent survey, the World Bank ranked it as the dominant barrier to continued growth. Ghana's main infrastructure challenge is power generation and it has some transportation issues. This problem is further compounded by a lack of technical expertise to deal with these problems. While education levels are improving, there are critical shortages in the sciences, technology, and vocational training.[73] Road transport is very important to Ghana's economy. It carries 96 percent of passenger and freight traffic.[74] Ghana's infrastructure needs are approximately $2.3 billion through 2021. Ghana currently spends $1.2 billion on infrastructure. This is approximately 7.5 percent of GDP. It loses $1.1 billion a year in inefficiencies. A large percentage of this shortfall comes from the underpricing of power. There is

---

[71]African Development Bank and African Development Fund, Country Operations Department West 1 Region, *Republic of Ghana Country Strategy Paper 2012-2016,* http://www.afdb.org/fileadmin/ uploads/afdb/Documents/Project-and-Operations/Ghana%20-%20CSP%202012%20-%202016.pdf, 1-2.

[72]Freedom House, "Map of Freedom 2014," http://www.freedomhouse.org/sites/default/files/ MapofFreedom2014.pdf (accessed February 23, 2014).

[73]African Development Bank and African Development Fund, Country Operations Department West 1 Region, *Republic of Ghana Country Strategy Paper 2012-2016,* 6-7.

[74]Ghana Investment Promotion Centre, "Infrastructure – Transportation," GIPC, http://www.gipcghana.com/invest-in-ghana/why-ghana/infrastructure/transportation-infrastructure.html (accessed February 23, 2014).

a net shortfall in funding of $0.4 million a year primarily related to water and power generation.[75] It is worth noting that Ghana's lack of investment in power generation held back GDP growth by 0.5 percent while roads did not have a major impact in growth.[76] The United States Agency for International Development's Power Africa program is leveraging private sector capabilities to execute multiple projects in Ghana. These include an 800 megawatts of thermal power generation capability which will require an investment of $0.8 billion, developing a gas fired power plant to produce 450 megawatts, and building biomass capabilities to name a few.[77] Ghana has identified that one area of opportunity to optimize growth is by maximizing foreign aid. Ghana seeks to have foreign aid reward as many contracts as possible to local firms in order to maximize the effect on the national skill base.[78] This recalibration of foreign aid could have a large impact on growth. In 2005, Ghana received $1.15 billion in net official development assistance.[79] Using these figures, Ghana could construct 378 km of two lane highways in order to meet transportation needs. However, since Ghana already enjoys a high road density these resources may be better used in other areas.

[75]Vivien Foster, and Nataliya Pushak, Policy Research Working Paper 5600, *Ghana's Infrastructure A Continental Perspective*, March 2011, The World Bank Group, http://www-wds.worldbank.org/external/default/WDSContentServer/WDSP/IB/2011/03/17/000158349_201103171459 09/Rendered/PDF/WPS5600.pdf (accessed February 23, 2014), 1-2.

[76]Ibid., 4.

[77]US Agency for International Development, "Private Sector," http://www.usaid.gov/powerafrica/ partners/private-sector (accessed April 11, 2014).

[78]African Development Bank and African Development Fund, Country Operations Department West 1 Region, *Republic of Ghana Country Strategy Paper 2012-2016,* 11.

[79]African Development Bank Group, *AfDB Statistics Pocketbook,* vol. 15, http://www.afdb.org/ fileadmin/uploads/afdb/Documents/Publications/The%20AfDB%20Statistics%20Pocketbook%202013.pdf (accessed February 23, 2014), 67.

VIGNETTE 2: RWANDA

Rwanda's development goal is to achieve the status of a low-income country by 2020. Rwanda has made impressive strides, but still suffers from major shortcomings in transport, energy, and poor national and regional connectivity. Rwanda is ranked 101 out of 142 nations in the Global Competitiveness Index for infrastructure development. Rwanda's power tariff is $0.18 per killowat hour as compared to $0.10-1.12 per killowat hour for the rest of its region. Transport costs are almost double those of regional rate. Rwanda's regional integration is fundamental to its continued prosperity. It is a relatively small landlocked country that requires access to the sea for its markets.[80] Rwanda will not only need to build its physical national infrastructure, it will also need to develop the skills necessary to maintain the infrastructure once it is constructed. Rwanda recognizes this need and has established it as a priority to develop human resources that have the skills to manage the national infrastructure.[81] In 2005, Rwanda received approximately $577 million in net official development assistance.[82] Rwanda could potentially construct up to 198 km of roadway each year. Rwanda is sorely lacking in transportation infrastructure so this would be a blessing. However, in Rwanda's case, this figure might be drastically reduced. This is due to Rwanda's geography. Rwanda is known as the land of *"mille collines "*or the land of a 1,000 hills.[83] In order to build infrastructure in this environment it will require a more intensive effort and will likely increase costs.

---

[80]African Development Bank and African Development Fund, Regional Department East A (OREA), *Rwanda Bank Group Country Strategy Paper 2012-2016,* October 2011, African Development Bank Group. http://www.afdb.org/fileadmin/uploads/afdb/Documents/Project-and-Operations/ Rwanda%20-%20CSP%202012-2016.pdf (accessed February 25, 2014), 2-3.

[81]Republic of Rwanda, Ministry of Infrastructure, *National Energy Policy and National Energy Strategy 2008-2012,* January 16, 2014, European Union Energy Initiative Partnership Dialogue Facility, http://www.euei-pdf.org/sites/default/files/files/field_pblctn_file/EUEI%20PDF_Rwanda_Energy% 20Policy%202008-2012_Final_Jan%202009_EN.pdf (accessed March 1, 2014), 7.

[82]African Development Bank Group, *AfDB Statistics Pocketbook,* XV: 101.

[83]Lathrop interview.

VIGNETTE 3: SENEGAL

Senegal resembles Ghana in regards to its commitment to infrastructure development. This commitment is possible due to the strong and persistent economic improvement and political stability. Senegal has been a stable democracy since the early 1980s.[84] While the situation is generally positive, there are significant aspects that will inhibit growth if infrastructure needs are not aggressively pursued. Senegal has submitted a Priority Roads Plan worth 2.4 billion euros. It is increasing regional integration by building roads to two neighboring countries, expanding airport and maritime port facilities, and building bridges across major waterways.[85] Investment in transport infrastructure will also help Senegal realize its tourism and mining potential, which are major drivers of the economy. Tourism accounts for 4 percent of GDP and mining accounted for 13 percent of exports.[86] The importance of infrastructure development in Senegal can be seen by the portfolio managed by the Africa Development Bank. In total, infrastructure needs accounted for 67.5 percent of the portfolio. Forty percent was designated for transport and energy while water and sanitation accounted for the other 34.5 percent.[87] Finally, Senegal's potential to become a regional infrastructure hub is being planned. Recent major products include the Tambacounda-Kedougou regional road and the 60 km Thiès-Seo-Diourbel tourism road. There are also plans to build transport networks from Dakar, Senegal to Bamako, Mali and from Dakar, Senegal to Conakry, Guinea.[88] These routes will provide transportation along the west coast of Africa

---

[84]African Development Bank and African Development Fund, Country Operations Department West Region, *Republic of Senegal, Country Strategy Paper 2010-2015,* September 2010, African Development Bank Group, http://www.afdb.org/fileadmin/uploads/afdb/Documents/Project-and-Operations/SENEGAL%20-%202010-2015%20CSP.pdf (accessed March 1, 2014), 2-3.

[85]Ibid., 12.

[86]Ibid., 13.

[87]Ibid., 14.

[88]Ibid., 18.

through four nations and into the interior to Mali. In 2005, Senegal received approximately $698 million in net official development assistance.[89] By using 20 percent of reported funds, Senegal could construct approximately 240 km of roadways.

VIGNETTE 4: TANZANIA

Tanzania is a leader in eastern Africa. It scores higher than most other east African nations in terms of civil liberties and political rights. The country has achieved impressive economic growth since the mid-1990s. While Tanzania has made good progress recently, significant challenges remain. Like other African countries examined, there are transport and energy shortages. Tanzania also suffers from a lack of skilled human resources due to a weak educational system.[90] Rail networks in Tanzania are poor and as a result, freight traffic has switched to the road networks. This is causing the degradation of an already stressed bitumen (commonly found in asphalt) road network.[91] The importance of the transport sector is highlighted by the fact that the largest programs the Africa Development Bank is supporting in Tanzania are major road construction projects. These are the 169 km Dodoma-Babati and the 39 km Tunduru-Mangaka road projects. A road project is also underway to help integrate Kenya with Tanzania.[92] Tanzania has approximately 86,472 km of roads for the entire nation. Of this total, the national government directly manages 33,891 km. This figure includes 12,786 km of

---

[89]African Development Bank Group, *AfDB Statistics Pocketbook*, XV:105.

[90]African Development Bank and African Development Fund African Development Bank, Regional Department East 1 (OREA). *United Republic of Tanzania, Country Strategy Paper 2011-2015*, June 2011. African Development Bank Group. http://www.afdb.org/fileadmin/uploads/afdb/Documents/ Project-and-Operations/TANZANIA-%202011-2015%20CSP.pdf (accessed March 2, 2014), 1-4.

[91]Ibid., 11.

[92]Ibid., 17.

trunk roads and 21,105 km of regional roads. Only 40 percent of the trunk roads and 4 percent of the regional roads are paved.[93]

Tanzania needs to dramatically increase its investment in infrastructure if it wants to reach the same level of development as the rest of developing nations. In order to do this, an annual investment of $2.4 billion would be required for a decade. More than one-third of this investment would go to the energy sector to relieve power shortages. Like Ghana, Power Africa is working with private industry on a variety of projects in Tanzania to increase energy capacity. These include the construction of biomass power generation facilities, wind farms, and hydroelectric projects to name a few.[94] In order to achieve the required level of spending, Tanzania would need to invest a little over 20 percent of GDP. The current investment rate stands at 9 percent of GDP or $1.2 billion. A large portion of this funding gap can be resolved by fixing inefficiencies in the system. This would relieve $500 million in the funding gap. However, even if the proper rates were charged, there were would still be a shortage of $700 million. While these adjustments and increased investment would be painful in the near term, they would yield positive results. Infrastructure investment currently contributes 1.3 percent to Tanzania's annual GDP growth. By investing the needed amount, growth rates would jump to 3.4 percent.[95] In 2005, Tanzania received $1.44 billion in net official development assistance.[96] Approximately 480 km of highway could be constructed using 20 percent of the foreign aid. This would increase the pave rate of the trunk road system by 4 percent. While this figure seems small, over the course of 10

---

[93]United Republic of Tanzania, Ministry of Works, "National Road Network," http://www.mow.go.tz/index.php/sectors/national-road-network (accessed April 1, 2014.

[94]US Agency for International Development, "Private Sector."

[95]Maria Shkaratan, Africa Infrastructure Country Diagnostic Country Report, *Tanzania's Infrastructure: A Continental Perspective* (Washington, DC: The World Bank, March 2010), African Development Bank Group, Africa Instructure Knowledge Program, http://infrastructureafrica.org/ system/files/library/2010/04/CR%20Tanzania.pdf (accessed March 2, 2014), 1-3.

[96]African Development Bank Group, *AfDB Statistics Pocketbook*, XV:121.

years it could almost double the pave rate for the national trunk road system. Additional monies could be reinvested in the road system as economic output increases due to the improvements in the national infrastructure. While encouraging, these costs must be closely watched.

CONCLUSION

From a standpoint of increasing the capabilities of the regional standby brigades, there is utility in establishing the engineer companies for each nation examined. While it would not eliminate the need for external support programs like ACOTA, this increased capacity and capability would provide needed engineer support for the standby brigade or a similar organization when it conducts operations across the continent. One potential shortfall that must be addressed in future is the dissolution of the unit after it is trained and equipped. It will take years for an African engineer unit to reach its full potential utilizing the current menu of programs. Efforts must be put in place on the front end of the process to ensure that high quality personnel are recruited and retained. In addition, incentives must be put in place to ensure that these individuals do not leave the service for a more lucrative civilian career. If an enduring unit capability is created, then this professional unit could form the core of a generating unit within the selected African military.

There is a more limited prospect of having the proposed engineer units making a demonstrable impact on civilian infrastructure. In Ghana, the impact would be negligible at best. Ghana already has a large amount of civilian development assistance and a comparatively high rate of road density compared to the other nations studied. Senegal and Tanzania receive a large amount of foreign aid but their road density is low. This engineer unit could be used to help maintain the small amount of road networks that are currently in place. They could also be used to help construct the areas mentioned above that facilitate tourism and regional integration. Rwanda stands to gain the most from the development of this capability. It is a small landlocked nation, it has limited national transport and energy infrastructure, and it requires regional access

39

to import and export goods. The establishment of a military engineer unit in this nation could have a positive effect in developing the nation's infrastructure and promoting regional economic growth. One area where military sources could help is with creating a special category for the International Military and Exchange and Training Program. A constant need was identified across all countries for technical engineering skills.

Overall, the assessment is there is potential in the development of this capability, especially for smaller nations like Rwanda. However, this study has only demonstrated the planning potential at the strategic and operational levels. There are considerations at the tactical level that have the potential to present friction that may be insurmountable. For example, as a rule, many individuals who have experience with engineer equipment state that it is extremely unreliable and costly to repair. Even if successful training programs are developed between the State Department and DOD, sufficient funding must be provided for the African engineer units to maintain their assigned equipment over the long run. Another potential source of efficient development is to have African engineers learn how to do construction management. This skill would be particularly valuable in nations such as Ghana that have demonstrated the ability to develop a robust transportation infrastructure. However, as the example in Tanzania shows, as part of this management effort, programs must be developed and implemented to minimize corruption. If this is not mitigated, then the entire program may prove unfeasible. For example, a recent historical study of road construction costs in sub-Saharan Africa from 1994-2010 showed that from 2005-2010 road construction costs increased from $316,000 per unit (the term unit is not quantitatively defined in the article) to $889,650. Not surprisingly, it was reported that openness in bidding processes and examining construction costs lowered overall expenses in 2010.[97]

The points raised above are but a sampling of considerations at the tactical level. In order to determine the feasibility of this approach and guide future research, it is recommended that a joint military and interagency group be formed at the geographic combatant command, Africa Command, and examine the efficacy of establishing an engineer unit capable of developing surface transport and providing power. If their conclusions reinforce the findings in this monograph then training and equipping program could be developed and rapidly implemented using a 1206 style program. A variety of engineer units from the Army, Navy, Air Force, and to a limited extent, the Marine Corps could provide the needed training. In the final analysis, this engineer capacity proposal will be of marginal benefit when one looks at the continent as a whole. Other programs such as the MCC and Power Africa that leverage private sector capabilities have a much larger effect. Nevertheless, the combatant commander may find that small contributions from American military engineers may help these nations achieve modest levels of infrastructure development, better prepare the regional security brigades, and help the United States indirectly achieve its strategic interests on the continent of Africa. These results are worth considering as the United States military builds its theater security cooperation plans for sub-Saharan Africa.

---

[97]Bilham Kimati, "Tanzania: Corruption Detected in Inflated Road Construction Project Costs," Tanzania Daily News, last modified July 3, 2012, All Africa, http://allafrica.com/stories/201207030466.html (accessed April 1, 2014).

BIBLIOGRAPHY

African Development Bank and African Development Fund. Country Operations Department West Region. *Republic of Senegal, Country Strategy Paper 2010-2015,* September 2010. African Development Bank Group. http://www.afdb.org/fileadmin/uploads/afdb/ Documents/Project-and-Operations/SENEGAL%20-%202010-2015%20CSP.pdf (accessed March 1, 2014).

_____. Country Operations Department West 1 Region. *Republic of Ghana Country Strategy Paper 2012-2016,* April 2012. African Development Bank Group. http://www.afdb.org/ fileadmin/uploads/afdb/Documents/Project-and-Operations/Ghana%20-%20CSP% 202012%20-%202016.pdf (accessed February 20, 2014).

_____. Regional Department East A (OREA). *Rwanda Bank Group Country Strategy Paper 2012-2016,* October 2011. African Development Bank Group. http://www.afdb.org/ fileadmin/uploads/afdb/Documents/Project-and-Operations/Rwanda%20-%20CSP% 202012-2016.pdf (accessed February 25, 2014).

_____. Regional Department East 1 (OREA). *United Republic of Tanzania, Country Strategy Paper 2011-2015,* June 2011. African Development Bank Group. http://www.afdb.org/ fileadmin/uploads/afdb/Documents/Project-and-Operations/TANZANIA-%202011-2015%20CSP.pdf (accessed March 2, 2014).

African Development Bank Group. *AfDB Statistics Pocketbook.* Vol. 15. http://www.afdb.org/ fileadmin/uploads/afdb/Documents/Publications/The%20AfDB%20Statistics%20Pocketb ook%202013.pdf (accessed February 23, 2014).

Africon. Summary of Background Paper 11. *Africa Infrastructure Country Diagnostic, Unit Costs of Infrastructure Projects in Sub-Saharan Africa,* June 2008. Infrastructure Trust Fund European Union Africa. http://www.eu-africa-infrastructure-tf.net/attachments/ library/aicd-background-paper-11-unit-costs-summary-en.pdf (accessed March 30, 2014).

Albright, Madeline, and Richard Williamson. "The United States and R2P: From Words to Action." The United States Institute of Peace, the United States Holocaust Memorial Museum, and the Brookings Institutue, 2013. http://www.brookings.edu/~/media/ Research/Files/Papers/2013/07/23%20united%20states%20responsibility%20protect%20 albright%20williamson/23%20united%20states%20responsibility%20protect%20albright %20williamson.pdf (accessed November 16, 2013).

Aldridge, Jennifer. "US Upgrades Senegalese Army Training Center." US Army Corps of Engineers. Last modified September 13, 2013. http://www.usace.army.mil/Media/ NewsArchive/StoryArticleView/tabid/232/Article/18243/us-upgrades-senegalese-army-training-center.aspx (accessed March 31, 2014).

Arieff, Alexis, Nicolas Cook, Lauren Ploch, Tiaji Salaam-Blyther, Alexandra Kendall, Curt Tarnoff, and Melissa D. Ho. Congressional Research Service Report for Congress. *U.S. Foreign Assistance to Sub-Saharan Africa: The FY2012 Request,* May 20, 2011. Federation of American Scientists. http://www.fas.org/sgp/crs/row/R41840.pdf (accessed October 14, 2013).

Armah, Stephen E. "Investigating the Influence of Political Stability of the Aid-Growth Relationship in Sub-Saharan Africa: A Panel Data Approach." *Journal of Economic Development, Management, IT, Finance, and Marketing* 2, no. 2 (September 2009): 32-56.

Batware, Billy. "The African Standby Force A Solution to African Conflicts?" European Peace University, December 19, 2011. Academia. http://www.academia.edu/3402412/The_African_Standby_Force_A_Solution_to_African_Conflicts (accessed January 2, 2014).

BBC. "African Troops for Mali 'in Days,'" January 15, 2013. British Broadcasting Corporation. http://www.bbc.co.uk/news/world-africa-21029916 (accessed January 3, 2014).

Birdsall, Nancy, and Alexis Sowa. "From Multilateral Champion to Handicapped Donor - And Back Again?" *PRISM* 4, no. 3 (2013): 73-87.

Bougheas, Spiros, Panicos O. Demetriades, and Edgar L. W. Morgenroth. "International Aspects of Public Infrastructure Investment." *The Canadian Journal of Economics/Revue canadienne d'Economique* 36, no. 4 (November 1, 2003): 884-910. http://www.jstor.org/stable/3131805 (accessed September 19, 2013).

Byman, Daniel. RAND Counterinsurgency Study Occasional Paper 3. "Understanding Proto-Insurgencies." National Defense Research Institute, 2007. RAND Corporation. http://www.rand.org/content/dam/rand/pubs/occasional_papers/2007/RAND_OP178.pdf (accessed November 24, 2013).

Collier, Paul, Anke Hoeffler, and Nicholas Sambanis. "The Collier-Hoeffler Model of Civil War Onset and the Case Study Project Research Design. " In *Understanding Civil War: Evidence and Analysis*. Vol. 1., edited by Paul Collier and Nicholas Sambanis, 7. Washington, DC World Bank, 2005.

Collier, Paul and Nicholas Sambanis, eds. *Understanding Civil War: Evidence and Analysis*. Vol. 1. Washington, DC World Bank, 2005.

Coulibaly, Souleymane, and Lionel Fontagné. "South-South Trade: Geography Matters." *Journal of African Economies,* July 8, 2004. CEPII. http://www.cepii.fr/PDF_PUB/wp/2004/wp2004-08.pdf (accessed February 24, 2014).

East African Community. "About EAC." Corporate Communications and Public Affairs Department. http://www.eac.int/index.php?option=com_content&view=article&id=1&Itemid=53 (accessed March 17, 2014).

Easterly, William. "Can the West Save Africa?" *Journal of Economic Literature* 47, no. 2 (June 2009): 373-447.

Economic Community of West African States. "Discover ECOWAS." ECOWAS. http://www.comm.ecowas.int/sec/index.php?id=about a&lang=en (accessed March 17, 2014).

Edelstein, David M. "Foreign Militaries, Sustainable Institutuions, and Postwar Statebuilding.*The Dilemmas of Statebuilding: Confronting the Contradictions of Postwar Peace*

Operations. Security and Governance Series, edited by Roland Paris and Timothy S. Sisk, 91. London: Routledge, 2009.

Foster, Vivien, and Nataliya Pushak. Policy Research Working Paper 5600. *Ghana's Infrastructure A Continental Perspective*, March 2011. The World Bank Group. http://www-wds.worldbank.org/external/default/WDSContentServer/WDSP/IB/ 2011/03/17/000158349_20110317145909/Rendered/PDF/WPS5600.pdf (accessed February 23, 2014).

Freedom House. "Map of Freedom 2014." http://www.freedomhouse.org/sites/default/files/ MapofFreedom2014.pdf (accessed February 23, 2014).

Ghana Investment Promotion Centre. "Infrastructure - Transportation." GIPC. http://www.gipcghana.com/invest-in-ghana/why-ghana/infrastructure/transportation-infrastructure.html (accessed February 23, 2014).

Herbst, Jeffrey Ira. *States and Power in Africa: Comparative Lessons in Authority and Control*. Princeton Studies in International History and Politics. Princeton, NJ: Princeton University Press, 2000.

IHS Jane's. *Jane's Sentinel Security Assessment - Central Africa, Ghana*. July 29, 2013. IHS, Inc. https://janes.ihs.com/CustomPages/Janes/DisplayPage.aspx?DocType=Reference&ItemI d=+++1305473&Pubabbrev=WAFR (accessed March 20, 2014).

_____. *Jane's Sentinel Security Assessment - Central Africa, Rwanda*. July 29, 2013. IHS, Inc. https://janes.ihs.com/CustomPages/Janes/DisplayPage.aspx?DocType= Reference&ItemId=+++1302631&Pubabbrev=CAF (accessed March 20, 2014).

_____. *Jane's Sentinel Security Assessment - Central Africa, Senegal*. July 29, 2013. IHS, Inc. https://janes.ihs.com/CustomPages/Janes/DisplayPage.aspx?DocType= Reference&ItemId=+++1305580&Pubabbrev=WAFR (accessed March 20, 2014).

_____. *Jane's Sentinel Security Assessment - Central Africa, Tanzania*. July 29, 2013. IHS, Inc. https://janes.ihs.com/CustomPages/Janes/DisplayPage.aspx?DocType= Reference&ItemId=+++1302683&Pubabbrev=CAF (accessed March 20, 2014).

International Action Network on Small Arms. Briefing Paper 107. *Africa's Missing Billions*, October 2007. Oxfam International. http://www.oxfam.org/sites/www.oxfam.org/files/ africas%20missing%20bils.pdf (accessed November 24, 2013).

International Institute for Strategic Studies. *The Military Balance 2012*. New York: Routledge, 2012.

Joint Chiefs of Staff. Joint Publication 3-34, *Joint Engineer Operations*. Washington, DC: US Government Printing Office, 2011.

Kapp, Lawrence, and Nina Serafino. Congressional Research Service Report for Congress. *The National Guard State Partnership Program: Background, Issues, and Options for Congress*, August 15, 2011. Federation of American Scientists. https://www.fas.org/sgp/crs/misc/R41957.pdf (accessed January 2, 2014).

Kimati, Bilham. "Tanzania: Corruption Detected in Inflated Road Construction Project Costs." Tanzania Daily News. Last modified July 3, 2012. All Africa. http://allafrica.com/stories/201207030466.html (accessed April 1, 2014).

Lathrop, Douglas. Retired Foreign Area Officer. Interview by author, Fort Leavenworth, KS, March 28, 2014.

Matthews, Captain Michelle. "Missouri Guardsmen Participate in Eastern Accord Exercise Kick off," September 6, 2012. Missouri National Guard. http://www.moguard.com/09-06-12-missouri-guardsmen-participate-in-eastern-accord-exercise-kick-off.html (accessed March 27, 2014).

Millennium Challenge Corporation. "Participating MCC Nations in Africa." http://www.mcc.gov/pages/countries/region/africa (accessed January 3, 2014).

_____. "Selection Criteria." http://www.mcc.gov/pages/selection (accessed October 14, 2013).

Montinari, Letizia, and Giorgio Prodi. "China's Impact on Intra-African Trade." *The Chinese Economy* 44, no. 4 (August 2011): 75-91.

North Dakota Office of the Adjutant General. *2009-2011 Biennial Report*. National Guard North Dakota. http://www.ndguard.ngb.army.mil/jointforce/Documents/NDNG-2009-11-Biennial-Report.pdf (accessed March 31, 2014).

Office of the Director of National Intelligence Council. *Global Trends 2030: Alternative Worlds,* December 2012. National Intelligence Council. http://www.dni.gov/files/documents/GlobalTrends_2030.pdf (accessed October 1, 2013).

Purtell, Major Bryan. "Flintlock 11 Kicks Off February 21 in Senegal/Media Opportunities," February 3, 2011. Special Operations Command Africa Public Affairs, US Africa Command. http://www.africom.mil/Newsroom/Article/7979/flintlock-11-kicks-off-february-21-in-senegal-medi (accessed March 27, 2014).

Ramachandran, Vijaya. "Power and Roads for Africa," March 2008. Center for Global Development. www.cgdev.org/content/publications/detail/15659 (accessed October 14, 2014).

Republic of Rwanda, Ministry of Instructure. *National Energy Policy and National Energy Strategy 2008-2012,* January 16, 2014. European Union Energy Initiative Partnership Dialogue Facility. http://www.euei-pdf.org/sites/default/files/files/field_pblctn_file/EUEI%20PDF_Rwanda_Energy%20Policy%202008-2012_Final_Jan%202009_EN.pdf (accessed March 1, 2014).

Rodriguez, General David M., and Assistant Secretary Linda Thomas-Greenfield. "TRANSCRIPT: General Rodriguez on Security Cooperation in Sub-Saharan Africa," October 25, 2013. US Africa Command. http://www.africom.mil/Newsroom/Transcript/11406/general-rodriguez-on-security-cooperation-in-sub-saharan-africa (accessed November 8, 2013).

Savun, Burcu, and Daniel C. Tirone. "Exogenous Shocks, Foreign Aid, and Civil War." *International Organization* 66, no. 3 (Summer 2012): 363-393.

Serafino, Nina. Congressional Research Service Report for Congress. *Security Assistance Reform: 'Section 1206' Background and Issues for Congress*, April 19, 2013. Federation of American Scientists. http://www.fas.org/sgp/crs/natsec/RS22855.pdf (accessed November 14, 2013).

Shkaratan, Maria. Africa Infrastructure Country Diagnostic Country Report. *Tanzania's Infrastructure: A Continental Perspective*. Washington, DC: The World Bank, March 2010. African Development Bank Group, Africa Instructure Knowledge Program. http://infrastructureafrica.org/system/files/library/2010/04/CR%20Tanzania.pdf (accessed March 2, 2014).

United Nations. *Economic Development in Africa Report 2011, Fostering Industrial Development in Africa in the New Global Environment,* 2011. United Nations Conference on Trade and Development. http://unctad.org/en/docs/aldcafrica2011_en.pdf (accessed March 16, 2014).

_____. *Economic Development in Africa Report 2013, Intra-African Trade: Unlocking Private Sector Dynamism,* 2013. United Nations Conference on Trade and Development. http://unctad.org/en/PublicationsLibrary/aldcafrica2013_en.pdf (accessed March 16, 2014).

United Republic of Tanzania, Ministry of Works. "National Road Network." http://www.mow.go.tz/index.php/sectors/national-road-network (accessed April 1, 2014.

US Africa Command. "National Guard State Partnership Program." USAFRICOM. http://www.africom.mil/what-we-do/security-cooperation-programs/national-guard (accessed January 2, 2014).

US Agency for International Development. *Power Africa, Leveraging Partnerships to Increase Access to Power in Sub-Saharan Africa,* March 26, 2014. http://www.usaid.gov/sites/default/files/documents/1860/power-africa-overview.pdf (accessed April 11, 2014).

_____. "Private Sector." http://www.usaid.gov/powerafrica/partners/private-sector (accessed April 11, 2014).

_____. "U.S. Government Agencies." USAID. http://www.usaid.gov/powerafrica/partners/us-government-agencies (accessed May 11, 2014).

US Army Africa. "Western Accord 13 Begins Command Post Exercise." http://www.usaraf.army.mil/NEWS/NEWS_130628_wa2.html (accessed March 27, 2014).

US Army Corps of Engineers. "USACE Overview." US Army Corps of Engineers Headquarters. http://www.usace.army.mil/Portals/2/docs/USACE_101_April_2013.pdf (accessed January 2, 2014).

US Congress. Senate. *Statement of General Carter Hamm USA Commander, US Africa Command before the Senate Armed Services Committee,* March 7, 2013. US Africa

Command. http://www.africom.mil/Content/CustomPages/ResearchPage/pdfFiles/ 2013%20AFRICOM%20Posture%20Statment.pdf (accessed November 8, 2013).

US Department of State. "African Contingency Operations Training and Assistance ACOTA Program." Press Release|Fact Sheet. Last modified February 6, 2013. The Office of Website Management, Bureau of Public Affairs. http://www.state.gov/r/pa/prs/ps/ 2013/02/203841.htm (accessed February 22, 2014).

US European Command. "Africa Partnership Station Delivers Gift of Hope to Ghana," March 7, 2008. http://www.eucom.mil/article/20633/africa-partnership-station-delivers-gift-hope (accessed March 31, 2014).

US President. *National Security Strategy*, May 2010. The White House. http://www.whitehouse. gov/sites/default/files/rss_viewer/national_security_strategy.pdf (accessed November 16, 2013).

_____. *Sustaining U.S. Global Leadership: Priorities for 21st Century Defense*, January 2012. US Department of Defense. http://www.defense.gov/news/defense_strategic_ guidance.pdf (accessed November 8, 2013).

_____. *United States Strategy Toward Sub-Saharan Africa*, June 2012. The White House. http://www.whitehouse.gov/sites/default/files/docs/africa_strategy_2.pdf (accessed November 8, 2013).

The World Bank. "Fact Sheet: Infrastructure in Sub-Saharan Africa." The World Bank Group. http://web.worldbank.org/WBSITE/EXTERNAL/COUNTRIES/AFRICAEXT/0,,content MDK:21951811~pagePK:146736~piPK:146830~theSitePK:258644,00.html (accessed March 15, 2014).

The World Factbook. "Ghana." Central Intelligence Agency. https://www.cia.gov/library/ publications/the-world-factbook/geos/gh.html (accessed February 27, 2014).

_____. "Rwanda." Central Intelligence Agency. https://www.cia.gov/library/publications/the- world-factbook/geos/rw.html (accessed February 27, 2014).

_____. "Senegal." Central Intelligence Agency. https://www.cia.gov/library/publications/the- world-factbook/geos/tz.html (accessed February 27, 2014).

_____. "Tanzania." Central Intelligence Agency. https://www.cia.gov/library/publications/the- world-factbook/geos/tz.html (accessed February 27, 2014).